*Rosicrucian
Rules, Secret Signs,
Codes and Symbols*

By Franz Hartmann
H. Spencer Lewis
William Q. Judge
Paul Sedir

Copyright © 2020 Lamp of Trismegistus. All rights reserved. No part of this publication may be reproduced or transmitted in any form or by any means, electronic or mechanical, including photocopying, recording, or by any information storage and retrieval system, without permission in writing from Lamp of Trismegistus. Reviewers may quote brief passages.

ISBN: 978-1-63118-488-8

Esoteric Classics

Other Books in this Series and Related Titles

History and Teachings of the Rosicrucians by W W Westcott &c (978-1-63118-487-1)

Rosicrucians and Speculative Masonry in the Seventeenth Century (978-1-63118-489-5)

The Rosicrucian Chemical Marriage by Christian Rosenkreuz (978-1-63118-458-1)

Masonic and Rosicrucian History by M P Hall & H Voorhis (978-1-63118-486-4)

Qabbalistic Teachings and the Tree of Life by M P Hall (978-1-63118-482-6)

The Kabbalah of Masonry & Related Writings by E Levi &c (978-1-63118-453-6)

The Sepher Yetzirah and the Qabalah by M P Hall (978-1-63118-481-9)

Confessions of an English Opium-Eater by T De Quincey (978-1-63118-485-7)

The Poem of Hashish by A Crowley & C Baudelaire (978-1-63118-484-0)

Fortune-Telling with Dice by Astra Cielo (978-1-63118-466-6)

History, Analysis and Secret Tradition of the Tarot by Hall &c (978-1-63118-445-1)

Crystal Vision Through Crystal Gazing by Achad (978-1-63118-455-0)

Ancient Mysteries and Secret Societies by M P Hall (978-1-63118-410-9)

The Secrets of Enoch by Enoch (978-1-63118-449-9)

The Gospel of the Nativity of Mary by St. Matthew (978-1-63118-448-2)

Buddhist Psalms by Shinran (978-1-63118-465-9)

The Path of Light: A Manual of Maha-Yana Buddhism (978-1-63118-471-0)

Arcane Formulas or Mental Alchemy by W W Atkinson (978-1-63118-459-8)

The Machinery of the Mind by Dion Fortune (978-1-63118-451-2)

The Leadbeater Reader: A Selection of Occult Essays (978-1-63118-483-3)

The Human Aura: Astral Colors and Thought Forms (978-1-63118-419-2)

Audio versions are also available on Audible, Amazon and Apple

Table of Contents

Introduction…7

Rosicrucian Rules
By Franz Hartmann…9

The Duties of a Rosicrucian
By Franz Hartmann…13

Rosicrucian Symbols
By Franz Hartmann…15

The Rosicrucian Code of Life
By Harvey Spencer Lewis…27

Rosicrucian Jewels
By Franz Hartmann…35

Rosicrucian "Orders"
By Franz Hartmann…37

The Society of the Rosicrucians
By William Q. Judge…53

The Secret Signs of the Rosicrucians
By Franz Hartmann…59

Secret Signs & Rosicrucian Rules
By Paul Sedir…67

INTRODUCTION

The word "esoteric" can be difficult to define. Esotericism in general can be seen less as a system of beliefs and more as a category, which encompasses numerous, different systems of beliefs. It's a bit of juxtaposition, since the word "esoteric" indicates something that few people know about, while the term itself broadly covers numerous philosophies, practices, areas of study and belief systems.

In a greater sense, Esotericism acts as a storehouse for secret knowledge, which is often considered ancient (by *tradition, if not by fact),* passed down from generation to generation, in private. At various times in history, simply possessing the knowledge of some of these subjects, was considered illegal and a jailable offence, if discovered. This usually included such general topics as Alchemy, Pharmacology, Qabalah, Hermeticism, Occultism, Ceremonial Magic, Astrology, Divination, Rosicrucianism and so on. Collectively, these areas of study were often referred to as the esoteric sciences.

Sometimes, the outer garment of a subject isn't esoteric, while what is hidden beneath it, is. As an example, Freemasonry isn't necessarily esoteric by nature (at *least not anymore),* but certain signs, passwords and handshakes given to the candidate during their initiation, are in fact, esoteric, in the sense that they are hidden from the general public.

Today, in the twenty-first century, such topics are readily available at bookstores across the country, and numerous mainsteam publishers offer beginners guides and coffee-table volumes on many of these subjects, intended for mass appeal. Books like *"The Secret"* have turned previously arcane topics into household knowledge. All that being the case, however, it isn't to say that there still aren't buried secrets to uncover, ancient wisdom being ignored and forgotten mysteries to be explored. In fact, it is often that we are only able to further our own studies by standing on the shoulders of these disappearing giants.

Lamp of Trismegistus is doing its part to help preserve humanity's esoteric history by making some of these classics available to those students who are seeking to unearth the knowledge of these ancient colossi.

So, be sure to check other titles from our *Esoteric Classics* series, as well as our *Occult Fiction, Theosophical Classics, Foundations of Freemasonry Series, Supernatural Fiction, Paranormal Research Series, Studies in Buddhism* and our *Christian Apocrypha Series.* You can also download the audio versions of most of these titles from Amazon, Apple or Audible, for learning on the go.

ROSICRUCIAN RULES

By Franz Hartmann

1. Love God above all.

> To "love God" means to love wisdom and truth. We can love God in no other way than in being obedient to Divine law; and to enable us to exercise that obedience conscientiously requires knowledge of the law, which can only be gained by practice.

2. Devote your time to your spiritual advancement.

> As the sun without leaving his place in the sky sends his rays upon the earth to shine upon the pure and the impure, and to illuminate even the most minute material objects with his light; likewise the spirit of man may send his mental rays into matter to obtain knowledge of all terrestrial things; but there is no need that the spirit should thereby lose its own divine self-consciousness, and be itself absorbed by the objects of its perception.

3. Be entirely unselfish.

> Spiritual knowledge begins only where all sense of self ceases. Where the delusion which causes man to imagine himself to be a being separated and isolated from others

ends, there he begins to realize his true state as an all-embracing universal and divine self-conscious power.

4. Be temperate, modest, energetic, and silent.

> The door to the inner temple is called "Contentment"; but no animal can enter therein, only he who walks uprightly, being conscious of his true dignity as a human being. Without energy, nothing can be accomplished; and only in the silence, when all thoughts and desires are at rest, can the Divine harmonies penetrate to the internal ear.

5. Learn to know the origin of the METALS contained within thyself.

> Ignorance is the cause of suffering. That which is material must be crucified and die, so that that which is spiritual may be resurrected and live.

6. Beware of quacks and pretenders.

> He who claims to be in possession of knowledge knows nothing; only he through whom the Word of wisdom speaks is wise.

7. Live in constant adoration of the highest good.

> The worm seeks for pleasure among abomination and

filth; but the free eagle spreads his wings and rises up towards the sun.

8. Learn the theory before you attempt the practice.

> He who travels with a trustworthy guide will be safer than he who refuses to profit by the experience of another.

9. Exercise charity towards all beings.

> All beings are one in the spirit; divided from each other merely by the illusion of form. He who is charitable towards another form in which the universal One Life is manifest, saves suffering to his own self.

10. Read the ancient books of wisdom.

> Books are to the unripe mind that which the mother's milk is to the nursling. We must receive drink from others until we have gained sufficient strength and experience to descend to the living fountain within ourselves, and to draw from there the water of truth.

11. Try to understand their secret meaning.

> That which is external may be seen with the external eye; but that which is spiritual can only be seen with the eye of the spirit.

These are the eleven rules which ought to be followed by those who desire to enter the temple of the Rosy Cross; but the Rosicrucians have a twelfth rule, an Arcanum, in which great powers reside, but of which it is not lawful to speak. This Arcanum will be given to those who deserve it, and by its aid they will find light in the darkness, and a guiding hand through the labyrinth. This Arcanum is inexpressible in the language of mortals, and it can, therefore, only be communicated from heart to heart. There is no torture strong enough to extract it from the true Rosicrucian; for even if he were willing to reveal it, those who are unworthy of it are not capable of receiving it.

THE DUTIES OF A ROSICRUCIAN

By Franz Hartmann

Those who are dead in the flesh will read the following with the external understanding; those who live in the spirit will see its internal meaning, and act accordingly.

The duties of a true Rosicrucian are:—

1. To alleviate suffering and to cure the sick without accepting any remuneration.

> The medicine which they give is more valuable than gold; it is of an invisible kind, and can be had for nothing everywhere.

2. To adopt the style of their clothing to the costumes of the country wherein they reside for the time being.

> The clothing of the spirit is the form which he inhabits, and must be adapted to the conditions of the planet whereon he resides.

3. To meet once a year in a certain place.

> Those who do not meet at that place, when their terrestrial career is over will have their names taken out of the book of life.

4. Each member has to select a proper person to be his successor.

> Each man is himself the creator of that being whose personality he adopts on the next step on the ladder of evolution.

5. The letters R.C. are the emblem of the order.

> Those who have truly entered the order will bear the marks upon their body, which cannot be mistaken by him who is capable of recognizing them.

6. The existence of the Brotherhood is to be kept secret for one hundred years, beginning from the time when it was first established.

> Nor will the "hundred years" be over until man has awakened to the consciousness of his own divine nature.

ROSICRUCIAN SYMBOLS

By Franz Hartmann

SIGNS FROM THE HEART OF THE CELESTIAL MOTHER

(*From the work of Antonio Ginther. August Vindelicorum. 1741.*)

Prænesis. A ship in the open sea, with a floating anchor, and a star shining overhead, with the inscription: *Hac monstrante viam.*

Emblema 1. An open book with the name MARIA, and a heart transfixed by a sword, with the inscription: *Omnibus in omnibus.*

2. A seven-headed monster threatened with a club. Inscription: *In virtute tua.*

3. A closed and sealed door with an angel attempting to open it. Inscription: *Signatur ne perdatur.*

4. A landscape representing an island. The sun rises and the stars shine. Inscription: *Aurora ab lacrymis.*

5. An orange tree bearing fruits, of which the inner part is sweet, while the rind is bitter. Inscription: *Dulce amarum.*

6. An altar with a fire upon it, in which a heart is burning, sending out a sweet odour. Inscription: *In odorem suavitatis.*

7. A pure white lily in a flower-pot, standing in a garden. Inscription: *Virginei laus prima pudoris.*

8. An angel separating wheat from chaff by means of a sieve. Inscription: *Dimittit inanes.*

9. A ring with a jewel exhibited upon a table. Inscription: *Honori invincem.*

10. A globe illuminated by the full moon. Inscription: *Plena sibi et aliis.*

11. Jacob's ladder with seven steps, reaching from the earth up to heaven. Inscription: *Descendendo ascendendo.*

12. A sun-dial attached to the wall of a tower. Inscription: *Altissimus obnumbrat.*

13. The signs of the Zodiac, with the sun passing through the sign of the Virgin. Inscription: *Jam mitius ardet.*

14. A hen brooding in a stable, brooding over eggs. Inscription: *Parit in alieno.*

15. Two palm-trees, inclined towards each other. Inscription: *Blando se pace salutant.*

16. A grape-vine, cut from the trunk, is weeping. Inscription: *Ut gaudeas mero.*

17. A plant, representing a myrrh. Inscription: *Amara sed salubris.*

18. A painter's easel, with a cloth ready for painting. Inscription: *Qua forma placebit.*

19. A heart transfixed by a sword. Inscription: *Usque ad divisionem animæ.*

20. Two doves pecking at each other. Inscription: *Amat et castigat.*

21. A passion flower. Inscription: *Delectat et cruciat.*

22. Wolves and sheep, eagles and bats, basking together in the sunshine. Inscription: *Non possentibus offert.*

23. A bird, sitting between thorns and thistles. Inscription: *His ego sustentor.*

24. Ivy winding around a dead tree. Inscription: *Nec mors separavit.*

25. Two hearts in a winepress. Inscription: *Cogit in unum.*

26. A crocodile shedding tears while eating a man. Inscription: *Plorat et devorat.*

27. Wolf devouring a sheep. Inscription: *Non est qui redimat.*

28. Tulips inclining toward the rising sun. Inscription: *Languexit in umbra.*

29. Two stringed musical instruments; a hand plays upon one. Inscription: *Unam tetigis se sat est.*

30. A white lily growing between thorns. Inscription: *Transfixum suavius.*

31. The prophet Jonah thrown into the raging sea. Inscription: *Merger ne mergantur.*

32. The setting sun and the evening star. Inscription: *Sequitur deserta cadentem.*

33. A cross with a snake wound around it. Inscription: *Pharmacumnon venenum.*

34. Eagle, rising towards the sun. Inscription: *Ad te levavi oculos.*

35. A squirrel standing upon a log, floating in the water and rowing. Inscription: *Ne merger.*

36. Light tower, illuminating the ocean. Inscription: *Erantibus una micat.*

37. Rock standing in a stormy sea. Inscription: *Non commovebitur.*

38. A diamond exposed upon a table. Inscription: *In puritate pretium.*

39. Grafting a tree. Inscription: *Accipit in sua.*

40. A man hanging upon a tree. Inscription: *Non est hac tutior umbra.*

41. A flock of sheep, each one bearing the letter T upon the forehead. Inscription: *Non habet redargutionem.*

42. Chandelier with seven lights. Inscription: *Non extinguetur.*

43. A solar eclipse. Inscription: *Morientis sideris umbra.*

44. The setting sun and a rainbow shedding tears. Inscription: *Desinit in lacrymas.*

45. Cypress blown at by winds coming from the four quarters of the world. Inscription: *Concussio firmat.*

46. Two hearts surrounded by thorns, with nails and a dagger. Inscription: *Vulneratum vulnerat.*

47. A heart transfixed by a sword and instruments of torture. Inscription: *Superminet omnes.*

48. Beehive, and bees flying around flowers. Inscription: *Currit in odorem.*

49. A chemical furnace with retorts, from which drops are falling. Inscription: *Color elicit imbres.*

50. A man sowing grain into furrows. Inscription: *Ut surgat in ortum.*

51. A cloth spread upon a field and sprinkled with water. Inscription: *A lacrymis candor.*

52. Ocean waves and a bird flying through the furrows of water. Inscription: *Mersa non mergitur.*

53. Noah's dove with an olive branch. Inscription: *Emergere nuntiat orbem.*

54. Flying eagle carrying a lamb. Inscription: *Tulit prædeam tartari.*

55. Rain descending upon flowers. Inscription: *Dulce refrigerium.*

56. Plumb-line and level. Inscription: *Recta a recto.*

57. A hot iron upon an anvil. Inscription: *Dum calet.*

58. Solitary bird sitting in a cave. Inscription: *Gemit dilectum suum.*

59. Elephant drinking blood flowing from a grape. Inscription: *Acuitur in prælium*.

60. Bird escaping from a nest. Inscription: *Ad sidera sursum*.

61. Sunrise rays shining into a heart of adamant. Inscription: *Intima lustrat*.

62. A flying bird attached to a string. Inscription: *Cupio dissolvi*.

63. Two birds of Paradise flying upwards. Inscription: *Innixo ascendit*.

64. A triple crown made of silver, iron, and gold. Inscription: *Curso completo*.

65. The statue of Dagon thrown down and broken to pieces. A corpse. Inscription: *Cui honorem honorem*.

66. The Red Sea dividing for the passage of the Israelites. Inscription: *Illue iter quo ostendum*.

67. Labyrinth with a human figure therein. A hand extended from heaven holds a thread reaching down to the figure. Inscription: *Hac duce tuta via est*.

68. A camp. Among the tents is a standard bearing the image of a man. Inscription: *Præsidium et decus*.

69. A clock, whose finger points to the second hour. Inscription: *Ultima secundo*.

70. Ship at sea carrying a light. Fishes and birds are attracted by the glow. Inscription: *Veniunt ad lucem*.

Epilogus.—Noah's ark in tranquil water. Inscription: *Non mergitur, sed extollitur*.

SIGNS REFERRING TO THE DIVINE CHILD

(From the above-mentioned work.)

Prænesis.—A hen with chickens under her wings. A hawk preying in the air above. Inscription: *Sub umbra alarum tuarum.*

Emblema 1. A figure kneeling and holding a book wherein is represented a fiery heart. Inscription: *Tolle lege.*

2. Altar upon which a fire is lighted by a sunray. Inscription: *Extinctos suscitat ignes.*

3. Sunray falling through a lens and setting a ship on fire. Inscription: *Ignis ab Primo.*

4. Sun shining upon a lambskin extended upon the earth. Inscription: *Descendit de cœis.*

5. A chrysalis upon a leaf. Inscription: *Ecce venio.*

[*no.6 has been lost*]

7. The sea and the rising sun. Inscription: *Renovabit faciem terræ.*

8. A rising sun eclipsed by the moon. Inscription: *Condor ut exorior.*

9. A chicken and an eagle in the air. The former is protected against the latter by a shield. Inscription: *A facie persequentis.*

10. A rose in the midst of a garden. Inscription: *Hæc mihi sola placet.*

11. A lamb burning upon an altar. Inscription: *Deus non despicies.*

12. Dogs hunting. Inscription: *Fuga salutem.*

13. A lamb dying at the foot of a cross.
Inscription: *Obediens usque ad mortem.*

14. The ark of the covenant. Rays of lightning.
Inscription: *Procul este profani.*

15. Sun in the midst of clouds.
Inscription: *Fulgura in pluvium fuit.*

16. Sun shining upon sheep and wolves.
Inscription: *Super vobos et malos.*

17. A well and a pitcher. Inscription: *Hauriar, non exhauriar.*

18. Animals entering the ark. Inscription: *Una salutem.*

19. Shepherd carrying a lamb. Inscription: *Onus meum leve.*

20. Sheep drinking at a well. The water is stirred by a pole.
Inscription: *Similem dant vulnera formam.*

21. A dove sitting upon a globe. Inscription: *Non sufficit una.*

22. Light penetrating the clouds.
Inscription: *Umbram fugat veritas.*

23. A vineyard and the rising sun.
Inscription: *Pertransiit beneficiendo.*

24. Three hearts with a sieve floating above them.
Inscription: *Cælo contrito resurgent.*

25. Swan cleaning his feathers before proceeding to eat.
Inscription: *Antequam comedum.*

26. A hungry dog howling at the moon.
Inscription: *Inanis impetus.*

27. Ark of the covenant drawn by two oxen.
Inscription: *Sancta sancte.*

28. A winepress. Inscription: *Premitur ut exprimat.*

29. An opening bud. Inscription: *Vulneribus profundit opes.*

30. Amor shooting arrows at a heart.
Inscription: *Donec attingam.*

31. Cross and paraphernalia for crucifiction.
Inscription: *Præbet non prohibet.*

32. A sunflower looking towards the rising sun.
Inscription: *Usque ad occasum.*

33. Drops of sweat falling down in a garden.
Inscription: *Tandem resoluta venit.*

34. Sword protruding from the clouds.
Inscription: *Cædo noncedo.*

35. Hammer and anvil, a forge and a fire.
Inscription: *Ferendo, non feriendo.*

36. A ram crowned with thorns upon an altar.
Inscription: *Victima coronata.*

37. A sheep carrying animals.
Inscription: *Quam grave portat onus.*

38. A crucified person and a snake upon a tree.
Inscription: *Unde mors unde vita.*

39. A tree shedding tears into three dishes.
Inscription: *Et læsa medelam.*

40. A spring fountain. Inscription: *Rigat ut erigat.*

41. A heart offered to an eagle.
Inscription: *Redibit ad Dominum.*

42. A heart upon a cross surrounded by thorns, crowned with a laurel. Inscription: *Pignus amabile pacis.*

43. Bird persecuted by a hawk seeks refuge in the cleft of a rock. Inscription: *Hoc tuta sua sub antro.*

44. Target with a burning heart in the centre; Amor shooting arrows at it. Inscription: *Trahe mi post te.*

45. Pelican feeding her young ones with her own blood. Inscription: *Ut vitam habeant.*

[*no.46 has been lost*]

47. Phœnix sinking into the flames.
Inscription: *Hic mihi dulce mori.*

48. Blood from a lamb flowing into a cup.
Inscription: *Purgantes temperat ignis.*

49. Clouds from which proceed rays of lightning.
Inscription: *Lux recto fatumque noscenti.*

50. Eagle flying towards the sun.
Inscription: *Tunc facie ad faciem.*

Epilogus.- A hedgehog, having rolled in fruits, is covered with them. Inscription: *Venturi providus ævi.*

He who can see the ineaning of all these allegories has his eyes open.

THE ROSICRUCIAN CODE OF LIFE

By Harvey Spencer Lewis

The following rules are taken from old and modern manuscripts wherein certain regulations are set forth for the guidance of Rosicrucians who are devoting their entire lives to an idealization of the Order's principles. Perhaps only in some of the old monasteries of India, or those in Tibet, could one live strictly in accordance with all the ancient regulations; but those selected for publication here can be adopted by a great many of our members in the Occident. We know from practical experience that most of these can be adhered to by any man or woman without interfering with the necessary duties and obligations of present-day living.

We know, also, that most of our Officers and advanced members are living the Rosicrucian life in accordance with the rules suggested here, much to their own great advancement, the joy of their associates in family and business, and the betterment of mankind generally. It will profit you greatly to try adopting as many of these rules as possible.

1. Upon arising in the morning start the day with a prayer of thankfulness to God for the return of consciousness, because of the opportunities it affords to continue the Great Work and mission of your life. Face the geographical east, inhale fresh air with seven deep breaths, exhale them slowly with mind concentrated upon the vitality going to each part of

the body to awaken the psychic centers. Then bathe, and drink a glass of cold water before eating.

2. Upon retiring, and after conducting all psychic experiments scheduled for the night, or attending to any special psychic or Rosicrucian work contained in your weekly lesson or program, give thanks to God for the day and its fruits; ask the Cosmic Hosts to accept your psychic services while you sleep, to use your consciousness as they desire and, if it please God and the Masters to have you live another day on Earth, So Mote It Be! Then, with thoughts of love for all living beings, and a sense of peace and harmony with all the universe, close your eyes and fall asleep, visualizing your inner self in the consciousness of God.

3. Before each meal wash your hands clean and hold them, palms downward, over the plate of food for a fraction of a minute. Then mentally pray that the benediction of God be granted to the food you eat that it may be magnetized with the spiritual radiations from your hands, and thus greatly supply the needs of the body. Before eating the first morsel, say mentally: "May all who need food share with me what I enjoy, and may God show me how I may share with others what they have not."

4. Before accepting any blessing from the material world (whether purchased by money, labor, or exchange, or whether received as a gift), say mentally: "By the privilege of God I receive this and pray that it may help me better to fulfill my mission in life." This applies even to such things as clothing, personal requisites, periods of pleasure at the theatre, church,

musicals, etc., or even to such small things as books, helpful reading matter, etc., and of course includes the receipt of money as salary, commission, gifts, or otherwise.

5. Whenever any special blessing is received, such as long desired things from the material world of any nature, or a small or large luxury, or an unexpected piece of goodness, do not use or apply it to your own personal use in any way until you have retired to the silence somewhere for a few minutes to meditate and ask this question: "Have I truly deserved this blessing and is there any way in which I can share the benefit of it—directly or indirectly—with others or for the benefit of man?" Then wait for an answer from the Cosmic. If you receive no word that it is undeserved or should be shared, or passed on to another, then say: "I thank God and the Cosmic for this blessing; may I use it to the glory of my Soul."

6. If any special honor—military, governmental, political, social, or otherwise—is being conferred upon you, always act with the utmost humility, proclaim your unworthiness (for who is truly worthy of all things?) and with a mental resolution that it must not make you proud or selfish. Accept the blessing with a prayer of thankfulness and assert that, in the name of those whom you can serve better with such blessing, you receive it.

7. Never permit yourself to enter discussions of other persons' religious beliefs, except to point out the soundness, goodness, or possible benefits of certain doctrines and thereby show them the good that exists in all religions. Hold not your religious thoughts as superior. Speak well of them if need be, point out how they serve you, but do not create in the minds

of others the thought that they are in sin or error because of their beliefs. That religion is best for each which enables one to understand God and God's mysterious ways.

8. Be tolerant on all subjects and bear in mind that destructive criticism creates naught but sorrow. Unless you can constructively comment on matters, refrain from speaking.

9. Attempt no direct reforms in the lives of others. Discover in yourself what needs correction and improve yourself, that by the Light of your Life you may point the way to others.

10. Flaunt not your attainments, nor boast of your Rosicrucian knowledge. You may be a Rosicrucian as a member of the brotherhood, but as a Rosicrucian in knowledge and power, the greatest and highest among us is but a child of the studies and unworthy of Rosicrucian recognition. Proclaim yourself, not as a master, but as a Rosicrucian student—ever a student—eternally.

11. Seek to share what you can spare, daily, even if in small ways and meager amounts. Go out of your way to find where that which you can give or do will be a blessing to someone or many, and while performing this duty shun all personal glory and let it be known that you are simply "about the work of the Cosmic."

12. Accept no personal thanks for any blessings you bestow, any gift you give, or any help you render. When "thanks" are expressed it is customary to say: "Please thank me

not, for it is I who am grateful. I seek, and must seek, to serve and labor for the Cosmic; you have afforded me an opportunity. But, now the obligation to pass it on rests with you; may you, too, find an opportunity to serve someone else,"—or any other words indicative of this spirit.

13. Accept no gift of a material nature for any good you do unless you agree with yourself in the moment of accepting it, and so state to the giver, that you will divide the blessing with someone where it will continue to carry on its mission of relief and help. This is essentially necessary when the material gift is of such a nature— like money, food, clothing, etc.—that it can be divided and is a common necessity on the part of many.

14. Bear in mind that through your Rosicrucian Order you always have an open portal to help many, and that by sharing with them any blessings you pass on to others, who are fratres and sorores of the Order in need, the blessings which come to you, perhaps as a trustee of the Cosmic.

15. As you give so shall you receive! As each opportunity to give is seized upon with the utmost impulsiveness, so will future blessings, sought or required, be granted to you by the Cosmic. The greater the impulsiveness—with little thought as to personal sacrifice —the greater will be the compensation credited in the Cosmic.

16. Let not a day pass by without speaking to someone of the work of the Cosmic through the portal of the Rosicrucian Order. Each day make someone more familiar with its Great Work, not always by soliciting, not always by preachments, but

by simple statements of facts, simple demonstrations, and the kind word of recommendation,

17. Respect all persons, honor thy father and mother; be sympathetic to the sinful, helpful to the afflicted, and of service to the Cosmic. He is greatest among you who is the greatest servant unto all. Hence the Master of a Lodge and the Imperator are greatest, because they may be the greatest servants.

18. Provide now, while consciousness can assist you, to take care of those who may be dependent after your transition; and if you have no one who will require a share of your earthly possessions after your transition—or you have sufficient to more than do for them— be certain that you grant, in proper and legal manner, a disposition of some of your worldly blessings to the superior body of your Rosicrucian Order—the Supreme Grand Lodge—that it may be helped in the work it is doing for others.

19. Go to the assistance of any living being, regardless of race, creed, or color, when you can render direct or indirect aid in any emergency. If you cannot give aid in person, but can call or solicit aid, this, too, is imperative. In quiet and peace perform your work, render your service, and retire with as little recognition as possible.

20. Maintain one place in your home that is sacred to you and your Order. In it find peace and time for meditation daily. Profane it not with pleasures of the flesh, but sanctify it with your higher thoughts.

21. Give your support, moral or physical, to some church in your community, that it may have your help in carrying on the Great Work in its Light.

22. Assume no political office without properly and duly notifying all who may sponsor or support your attainment of your definite views and principles toward humanity at large, that they may not expect or depend upon your submission to principles of a lesser degree.

23. Judge not, unless you are so placed that those to be judged come legally and formally before you as an accredited servant of the multitude. Then in sympathy understand, in mercy comprehend, in leniency estimate, and with love be fair. For the Law of Compensation will make adequate demands, and the God of all is alone a truly competent judge of all facts.

24. Repeat no slander, tell no tales, and support no reports that injure or condemn unless accompanied by more than the same degree of constructive criticism and comment, and only after you have completely investigated and learned all the facts.

25. Seek the good in all things and give public praise to what you find. Look not upon the changing character of the outer self, but discover the real Self within. Learn to know all beings and love them.

26. Gamble not with the lot of another who in ignorance may lose and suffer what you gain.

27. Avoid all extremes in thought and act; be moderate in all desires, and subdue your passions in all directions.

28. Attempt no radical or sudden changes in the natural scheme of things; remember the Rosicrucian injunction: Not by revolution, but through evolution, are all things accomplished in permanency.

29. Hold sacred and above all criticism the ideals of the Rosicrucians. Permit no slander to affect the good name of your Order. Live that life which will prove the goodness of your principles. And be ready to defend the emblem of the Rosy Cross with the might of your life and the light of your being.

ROSICRUCIAN JEWELS

By Franz Hartmann

The most valuable jewel of the Rosicrucians is WISDOM, which is represented by a pure DIAMOND in the center of the ROSE, but the CROSS is adorned with twelve jewels of priceless value, in all of which the power that resides in the truth is manifested. These jewels are:

1. *Jasper* (dark green). The power of active light, multiplying itself to a sevenfold degree, and evolving seven states of the one light, by which the seven states of darkness may be consumed.

2. *Hyacinth* (yellow). LOVE, born from the matrix of Light, manifesting itself as it grows, and emitting red rays. Its power overcomes the spirit of anger and violence.

3. *Chrysolite* (white). Princely wisdom. It confounds that which is foolish and vain, subdues it, and comes out of the battle victorious.

4. *Sapphire* (blue). Truth; originating and growing out of its own essence. It overcomes doubt and vacillation.

5. *Smaragd* (green). The blooming spring in its eternal justice, destroying the unjust attributes of a perverted and degenerate nature, and opening the fountain of infinite treasures.

6. *Topaz* (golden). The symbol of peace, mild and pleasant. It suffers no impurity or division to exist, neither does

it admit that which causes separation and quarrels. It heals ruptures and cures wounds.

7. *Amethyst* (violet). Impartiality, equilibrium of justice and judgment. It cannot be falsified, bent, or counterfeited. It weighs all things in the scales of justice, and is opposed to fraud, cruelty, or tyranny.

8. *Beryl* (diverse colors). Meekness, humility; the equal temperature of the spirit, being kind and good, and overcoming wrath, stubbornness, and bitterness.

9. *Sardis* (light red). The high magical FAITH, growing into power, and destroying fear, skepticism, and superstition.

10. *Chrysoprase* (light green). Invisible power and strength, overcoming all opposition, allowing nothing to remain which could possibly resist the law.

11. *Sardonyx* (striped). Triumphant JOY and gladness, flowing from the eternal fountain of happiness, destroying all sorrow and sadness. (May it bless you !).

12. *Chalcedony* (striped). The crown of Victory, dominion, glory. The keystone and the greatest of all miracles, turning everything to the glorification of GOD.

THE ROSICRUCIAN "ORDERS"

By Franz Hartmann

Why is there so much perplexity about the mysterious order of the Rosicrucians? Let us ask in return, Why is there so much perplexity about that mysterious being called "Man"? The answer is that man is a spiritual being, inhabiting the spiritual world, which he has never entirely left; while the terrestrial personality in which he manifests himself during his earthly life is an inhabitant of this planet. That which the historian and the scientist know about man is merely that which refers to his physical body; while nothing is known to them about his real self. To imagine that such knowledge is true anthropology is like imagining that we know all about a man if we once see the coat which he wears. Likewise the true Rosicrucians, whether they still walk upon the earth in a visible form, or whether they inhabit the astral plane, are spiritual powers, such as are beyond the reach of examination of the externally reasoning historian or scientist. They are people who, as the Bible expresses it, "live upon the earth, but whose consciousness is in heaven." The vulgar sees only the external form, but not the spirit which is the true inhabitant of that form. To discern the latter, the power of spiritual discernment is required.

The coat which a man wears does not make the man; to pour water over a person does not make him a true Christian, and to have one's name entered into the register of some society calling itself "Rosicrucian," does not endow one with the rosy and golden light of love and wisdom that comes from the unfoldment of the "Rose" within the centre of one's soul. But it is far easier to undergo some external ceremony than to die the mystic death which is required for the purpose of passing through the "Gates of Gold"; it is easier to profess a creed than to acquire true knowledge; and for this reason we find during the Middle Ages not less than at this present time many people who imagine that they could be made into Rosicrucians and Adepts, by joining some society dealing with mystical subjects.

In the beginning of the 17th century Germany was overrun, not only by monks and nuns and religious fanatics of all kinds, but also by a great many impostors and adventurers. There were pretended Alchemists, Astrologers, Fortune-tellers, and there was a universal mania among the people to pry into the secrets of Nature, and to enrich themselves by alchemical processes, or, if need be, by the help of the devil.

This epidemic of superstition and folly seemed to require a strong remedy, and as foolish people are not accessible to reasonable arguments, it occurred to some sharp-witted mind to try the more caustic remedy of sarcasm. There appeared in the year 1614 two pamphlets, written by the same author, entitled, "Universal and General Reformation of the Whole Wide World," and the "Fama Fraternitatis; or, Brotherhood of the Laudable Order of the R.C. (Rosicrucians), a message to the Governments, nobles, and scientists of

Europe." This book was out of print during the last century, and Frederic Nicolai, in Berlin, had it reprinted in the year 1781, falsifying, however, its date, inserting 1681 instead of the correct date, and "Regensburg" instead of "Berlin." Another edition of the Fama Fraternitatis appeared at Frankfurt-on-Maine in the year 1827, and to this was added an additional part, entitled "Confessio."

These books, soon after they first appeared, made a great impression upon the public mind, and were immediately translated into several languages. The Universal Reformation is a satirical work. Its most interesting contents are an account of the meeting of a supposed Congress for the purpose of reforming the world. The story is as follows:—At the time of the Emperor Justinian, Apollo takes a look at the world, and finds it to be full of vices and wickedness. He therefore makes up his mind to call together a meeting of all the wise and virtuous men of the country to consult together how this evil might be remedied. Unfortunately, among all of them there is none to be found who is possessed of sufficient virtue and intelligence to give the desired advice. Apollo therefore assembles the seven ancient sages of Greece and three Romans, Marcus, Cato, and Seneca. A young Italian philosopher, by the name of Jacob Mazzonius, is appointed secretary.

The congregation meets in the delphic Palatium; and now follow the speeches which were held. The sages talk the most egregious nonsense. Thales, for instance, advises that a window should be inserted in the breast of every man, so that the people could look into his heart. Solon has become a communist, and wants to divide out all the public and private property, so that all should have equal parts. Bias proposes to prohibit all intercourse between the people, to destroy the bridges and to forbid using ships. Cato desires that God should be asked to send another deluge, to destroy the whole feminine sex and all males over 20 years of age; and to request Him to invent a new and better method of procreation. All the sages dispute and contradict each other, and finally it is resolved to cite the diseased century and make it come into court, so that the patient may be closely investigated. The century is brought in. It is an old man with a healthy-looking face, but having a weak voice. They examine him, and find that his face is painted, and a further investigation shows that not a single part of his body is without some disease. The savants then come to the conclusion that they cannot cure him; but they do not want to adjourn without having it appear that they had done something very useful and important, so they impose a new tax upon cabbage, carrots and parsley.

They publish the document with a great deal of swagger and self-praise, and the delighted people jubilate and applaud. The meaning of this pamphlet, which was written for the purpose of throwing ridicule upon a certain class of people who wanted to improve the world at once and to show the absurdity and impossibility of such an undertaking, was plain enough, and it seems incredible that its purpose should have been misunderstood. That there were any people who took the matter seriously shows the extreme ignorance and want of judgment of the common people of those times, and forms an interesting episode for the student of history and intellectual evolution. The other pamphlet which accompanied the former is the celebrated Fama Fraternitatis. The Universal Reformation threw ridicule upon the self-constituted "world-reformers," and this second pamphlet now invites these would-be reformers to meet, and it, at the same time, gives them some useful hints as to what they might do to attain their object; advising them that the only true method for improving the world is to begin by improving themselves. This pamphlet being like the other one, a satire upon the would-be reformers and so-called Rosicrucians, might, for all that, have been written by a genuine Rosicrucian, for it contains true Rosicrucian principles, such as are advocated by the Adepts. It shows the insufficiency of the scientific and theological views of those times.

It ridicules the imbecility of the pretended Alchemists, who imagined that by some chemical process they could transform lead into gold; but in doing so it gives good advice, and under the mask of divulging the laws and objects of some mysterious Rosicrucian Society, it indicates certain rules and principles, which afterward formed the basis of an organized society of investigators in Occultism, who adopted the name Rosicrucians.

Added to this, Fama Fraternitatis is the story of the "pious, spiritual, and highly-illuminated Father," Fr. R. C. Christian Rosencruetz. It is said that he was a German nobleman, who had been educated in a convent, and that long before the time of the Reformation he had made a pilgrimage to the Holy Land in company with another brother of this convent, and that while at Damascus they had been initiated by some learned Arabs into the mysteries of the secret science. After remaining three years at Damascus, they went to Fez, in Africa, and there they obtained still more knowledge of magic, and of the relations existing between the macrocosm and microcosm. After having also travelled in Spain, he returned to Germany, where he founded a kind of a convent called Sanctus Spiritus, and remained there writing his secret science and continuing his studies. He then accepted as his assistants, at first three, and afterwards four more monks from the same convent in which he had been educated, and thus founded the first society of the Rosicrucians. They then laid down the results of their science in books, which are said to be still in existence, and in the hands of some Rosicrucians. It is then said that 120 years after his death, the entrance to his tomb was discovered. A staircase led into a subterranean vault, at the door of which was written, Post annos CXX. patebo.

There was a light burning in the vault, which however, became extinct as soon as it was approached. The vault had seven sides and seven angles, each side being five feet wide and eight feet high. The upper part represented the firmament, the floor the earth, and they were laid out in triangles, while each side was divided into ten squares. In the middle was an altar, bearing a brass plate, upon which were engraved the letters, A. C. R. C., and the words, Hoc Universi Compendium vivus mihi Sepulchrum feci. In the midst were four figures surrounded by the words, Nequaquam Vacuum. Legis Jugum. Libertas Evangelii. Du Gloria Intacta. Below the altar was found the body of Rosencreuz, intact, and without any signs of putrefaction. In his hand was a book of parchment, with golden letters marked on the cover with a T (Testamentum?), and at the end was written, Ex Deo naximur. In Jesu morimur. Per Spiritum Sanctum reviviscimus." There were signed the names of the brothers present at the funeral of the deceased. In the year 1615, a new edition of these pamphlets appeared, to which was added another one, entitled Confessio; or, "the Confession of the Society and Brotherhood of the R. C.;" giving great promises about future revelations, but ending with the advice to everybody that until these revelations were made the people should continue to believe in the Bible.

All these pamphlets had—as will be shown farther on—one and the same author, and as the "General Reformation" was of an entirely satirical character and a pure invention, having no more foundation, in fact, than the Don Quixote de la Mancha of Cervantes, there is no reason whatever why we should believe that the succeeding pamphlets should have been meant seriously, and that the story of the returned knight, Christian Rosencreuz, should have been anything more than an allegory. Moreover, there is no indication of what became of the body of that knight after it was once discovered, nor that the temple of the Holy Ghost (Sanctus Spiritus) exists anywhere else but in the hearts of men. The whole object of these pamphlets seems to have been to present great truths to the ignorant, but to dish them up in a fictitious form, appealing to the curiosity of the people, and to the prevailing craving for a knowledge of the mysteries of Nature, which the majority of the people of these times wanted to know for the purpose of obtaining selfish and personal benefits. The beauty of the doctrines which shone through these satirical writings were so great and attractive that they excited universal attention; but at the same time the craving of the majority of the people for the mysterious was so great that it blinded their eyes, and rendered them incapable of perceiving the true object of the writer, which was to ridicule the pretensions of dogmatic science and theology, and to draw the people up to a higher conception of true Christianity.

The belief in the existence of a real secret organization of Rosicrucians, possessed of the secret how to make gold out of lead and iron, and of prolonging life by means of taking some fluid in the shape of a medicine, was universal; and quacks and pretenders of all kinds roamed over the country and helped to spread the superstitions, often selling worthless compounds for fabulous prices as being the "Elixir of Life;" while others wasted their fortunes and became poor in making vain efforts to transmute metals. A flood of writings appeared, some attacking and some defending the Rosicrucian Society, which was supposed to exist, but of which no one knew anything. Some people, and even some of the well-informed ones, believed in the existence of such a society; others denied it. But neither one class nor the other could bring any positive proofs for their beliefs. People are always willing to believe that which they desire to be true, and everyone wanted to be admitted as a member of that secret society, of which nobody was certain whether it existed at all; and if anyone boasted of being a Rosicrucian, or succeeded in creating the impression that he was one, he awed the ignorant, and was regarded by them as a very favored person, and in this way impostors and adventurers often succeeded in preying upon the pockets of the rich.

Those who wanted to be taught magic and sorcery desired that a society or school where they might learn such things should exist; and because they desired it they believed in its existence. If no genuine Rosicrucian could be found, one had to be invented. If the true Rosicrucian society was not to be had, imitations of what was believed to constitute a Rosicrucian society had to be organized. In this way numerous societies were formed, calling themselves "Rosicrucians"; and "Rosicrucianism" took various shapes. One of the most important publications, and which is calculated to throw light upon the mysterious subject of Rosicrucianism which still perplexes the learned, is the Chymical Marriage of Christian Rosencreutz, printed in 1616. This, again, was written to throw ridicule upon the vain and self-conceited dogmatists, scientists, and "gold-makers" of those times, while at the same time it contains high and exalted truths, disguised in an allegorical form, but easily to be perceived by the practical Occultist, and by him only. It can easily be seen that the style and tendencies of this publication have a great deal of resemblance to that of the Fama Fraternitatis. Now it has been ascertained beyond any doubt that the author of the "Chemical Marriage" was Johann Valentine Andreae, * who wrote it while a young student in the years 1602 and 1603 in Tübingen. He acknowledges this in the history which he gives of his life, and he adds that he intended to give a true picture of the popular follies of that time. This renders it extremely probable that he was also the author of the "General Reformation," of the Confessio, and of the story of

Christian Rosencreutz, and this probability amounts to almost conviction if we take into consideration the discovery made afterwards, that the "General Reformation" is nothing else but a literal translation of a part of a book from Boccalini Ragguagli di Parmaso.

Andreae was a great admirer of that author, and he also adopted his style in his Mythologia Christiana; it is therefore plain that he also made the above-named translation, and added it to his "Fama Fraternitatis." Both writings, in fact, form a complement to each other. In the "General Reformation" the political would-be-reformers are held up to ridicule, and in the "Fama" the mystical dreamers, imaginary theosophists, pretended gold-makers, and supposed discoverers of the universal panacea are castigated. There can be no reasonable doubt that this was Andreae's object, and, moreover, his intimate friend, Professor Besoldt, in Tübingen, acknowledged it in saying that the character of both books was plain enough, and that it was very strange that so many intelligent people had been led by the nose to mistake their meaning.

Andreae himself, without, however, acknowledging himself to be their author, expressed himself to the effect that the whole was a satire and a fable. In his "confession" he says: (Sc.) risisse semper Rosicrucianam fabulum et curiositatis fraterculos fuisse in sectatum † and in his paper entitled "Turris Babel, seu judiciorum de Fraternitatae Rosaccae crucis chaos," he speaks still more plainly upon this subject. It seems to have been his object in this latter publication to help those to become sober again who had become intoxicated by misunderstanding the former publications, for he exclaims: "Listen, ye mortals! In vain will ye wait for the arrival of that fraternity; the comedy is over. The fama has played it in, the fama has played it out," etc., etc. Still there were many who were not satisfied with this explanation, and who believed that it had been Andreae's intention to cause by his fama, a secret society of the scientists of his age to come into existence; but Andreae was too wise to attempt such an absurdity and to apply to the most unreasonable persons of his age to form a reasonable society. The question why he should have selected the name "Rosicrucian" for his imaginary society is not difficult to answer:

The Cross and the Rose were favorite symbols among the Alchemists and Theosophists long before anything of a "Rosicrucian Society" was known. Moreover, in his own coat of arms, as in that of Luther, there was a cross and four roses, a circumstance which probably led him to select that name. There is, perhaps, very rarely a fable or work of fiction invented which is not based upon some fact, however disconnected such facts may be with the subject. A work, entitled Sphinx Rosæa, printed in 1618, makes it appear very plausible that the writer of the Fama Fraternitatis, in inventing the story of Christian Rosencreutz and his three brothers, whose number was afterwards increased by four more, had certain originals in his mind, which served as prototypes to construct his story. The author of that Sphinx says that the idea of forming such a society for the general reformation of mankind arose from the success of Luther's Reformation; that the knight, Christian Rosencreutz, was, in reality, no other person than a certain

Andreas von Carolstadt, an adventurer, who had travelled a great deal, but never been in Palestine. He made himself so obnoxious to the clergy of his time, whom he desired to reform, that they, after his death, put the following Epitaph upon his grave:—Carolstadius Pestis Ecclesiae venonissima, tandem a Diabolo occisus est. This means: "Here lies Carolstadt, who was a poisonous plague to the Church until the devil killed him at last."

The three supposed associates of Rosencreutz were the friends of Carolstadt, the reformer Zwingli, Oecolompadius, and Bucerus, and the four others, who were supposed to have been added afterwards, were probably Nicalaus Palargus, Marcus Stubner, Martin Cellurius, and, finally, Thomas Münster, all of which persons were more or less known on account of their desire to aid in reforming the Church. As the people became infatuated with the idea of becoming Rosicrucians, and no real society of Adepts could be found, they organized Rosicrucian societies without any real Adepts, and thus a great many so-called Rosicrucian societies came into existence. There was one such society founded by Christian Rose in 1622, having head centers in the Hague, Amsterdam, Nuremberg, Mantua, Venice, Hamburg, Dantzig and Erfurt.

They used to dress in black, and wore at their meetings blue ribbons with a golden wreath and a rose. As a sign of recognition the brothers wore a black silk cord in the top button hole. This ornament was given to the neophytes after they had promised under oath to be strangled by such a cord rather than reveal the secrets which they were supposed to possess. They also had another sign, consisting of the "tonsure," such as is used today by the Roman Catholic clergy, meaning a small round shaven spot on the top of the head, originating probably from the custom of the Buddhist priests, who shave their whole head. Hence many of them wore a wig, in order not to be recognized as belonging to the brotherhood. They led a very quiet life, and were devout peoples.

On all high festivals, very early at sunrise they would leave their residence, and go out through the gate of the town facing the east. When another one of them appeared, or when they met at other places, one would say: Ave Frater! to which the other would answer, Rosae et Aureae; then the first one said Crucis, then both together said: Benedictus Deus Dominus noster, que nobis dedit Signum! They also had for the sake of legitimation a large document, to which the Imperator affixed the great seal. There was another "Rosicrucian society," formed at Paris in the year 1660 by an apothecary named Jacob Rose. This society was dissolved in 1674, in consequence of the notorious case of wholesale poisoning by the ill-reputed Marquise de Brinvillier Whether or not there ever were any real Adepts and genuine Alchemists among the members of these Rosicrucian societies, we are, of course, not in a position to affirm. We are satisfied to know that Adepts do exist and that Alchemy is a fact; but whether they had anything to do with these orders we do not know, nor do we care about it, as it is now of no consequence whatever.

All that we know for certain in regard to this matter is, that there existed at that time persons in possession of an extraordinary amount of occult knowledge, as is shown by the books they have left; but whether these persons belonged or did not belong to any organized society, is absolutely useless to know. During the life of Theophrastus Paracelsus, he was the intellectual center to which Alchemists, Occultists, Mystics, Reformers and Rosicrucians were attracted, but there is no indication that he was a member of any society of men calling themselves "Rosicrucians." There is, likewise, no indication that after the time of Paracelsus any organized society of true Adepts, calling themselves "Rosicrucian Society," ever existed. Some of the greatest minds of that age were engaged in occult research, and were naturally attracted together by the bonds of sympathy; but however much they may have been united in the spirit (in the temple of the Holy Ghost), there is no indication that they had an organized society on the external plane, nor would any real Adepts need any other but spiritual signs of recognition. A book printed in 1714, and written by Sinecrus Renatus, contains the remarkable information that some years ago the Masters of the Rosicrucians had gone to India, and that none of them at present remained in Europe. This is not at all improbable; for the moral atmosphere of Europe is at the present time not very congenial for spiritual development, nor very inviting to those who, while progressing on the Path of Light, are reincarnating in physical forms.

As all researches after a real Rosicrucian society consisting of genuine Adepts were naturally fruitless, the excitement caused by the Fama Fraternitatis gradually ceased, and there was not much said or written about them until between the years 1756 and 1768, when a new degree of

Freemasonry came into existence, called the "Rosicrucian Knights," or the order of Rose-croix, or the Knights of the Eagle and Pelican; but we should in vain search among these knights for any genuine Adept, or even for anyone possessed of occult knowledge or power; for as our modern churches have lost the key to the mysteries which were once entrusted to their guardianship, and have degenerated into places for social gatherings and religious pastime, so our modern Masons have long ago lost the Word, and will not find it again unless they dive below the surface of external ceremonies and seek for it in their own hearts.

THE SOCIETY OF THE ROSICRUCIANS

By William Q. Judge

The following are in outline the fundamental doctrines of the Brothers of the Rosy Cross. He who fulfills the required conditions, may find all necessary information in the " Book of Initiation," and they say that when he is ready he finds with ease, a guide who, through his *higher* instructs and directs him infallibly.

It is understood that the Society desires to be truly spiritual and asks no fees, but it seeks as members only those who are practical workers in the cause of humanity. But it is a secret body, not from fear of enemies, but in order to spread the truth, unimpeded by the war of opinions. The truth being eternal, is not subject to opinion, but to those who are able to see, it stands revealed in its own light.

1. The *Universe* as a whole is a *Unity,* having only *one,* eternal, universal and fundamental cause for its existence. All the multifarious forms, essences, powers or principles, are not originally self-existent, but are merely various manifestations of that one and universal cause. They are various modes of one original activity, and their shapes or organisms are the products of that activity, working upon different planes of existence and in various stages of evolution.

2. This cause, being eternal, unlimited and infinite, is beyond the power of the intellectual comprehension of any mortal and limited being. Its presence may be perceived everywhere, but in its highest aspect it can fully be known only to itself. Beings lower than itself, may intuitively feel its presence, but cannot intellectually know it, until they have risen up to its own level on the plane of existence. To avoid circumlocution, we call that eternal (spiritual) principle in its highest aspect "*God*" or "*Brahm*"; both words signifying originally "Good."

3. In this eternal and universal cause, the center or fountain of *All*, is contained potentially everything existing in the Universe. It is itself, germinally or in a more or less developed state contained in everything that exists, It forms the (spiritual) center of every living organism, and life itself is only a mode of manifestation of its own power. It is the cause and the architect of every form; it builds the form which it inhabits, from that center, by the power of its own (consciously or unconsciously active) *will* and *thought*, and by the means offered by eternal nature, the latter being itself a product of previous states of its own existence and eternal action.

4. The highest form of activity of this principle requires for its perfect expression, perfect means. The perfect cannot manifest its perfection in an imperfect organism. The place which a being occupies on the ladder of evolution, depends on the progress which that divine principle, acting in the center of each being, has made in evolving an organism, adapted to its manifestation.

5. The most perfect organism for the manifestation of the divine and universal principle in its highest aspect, of which we know, in the (spiritual) organism of Man. In this organism, this divine principle, after having attained *sensation* and *consciousness* in the lower forms of nature, may acquire (spiritual) *self-consciousness* and *self-knowledge,* evolving what is called the individual *mind,* with all its powers and faculties, for (spiritual) perception and *real knowledge* or wisdom.

6. The (ordinarily) visible so called physical-body of man is not the *real* Man, but merely a more or less imperfect representation of the real, or "inner man," whose sphere of activity may extend as far as the sphere of his mind; in other words—as far as the power of his (spiritual) perception. The "inner man " is a reality, which after having attained—by the power of self-differentiation—an individual existence, will retain its individuality, after the physical forms, which it has occupied for the purposes of evolution during its life upon a planet, have been disintegrated and changed into other forms.

7. Every being continues to exist in its essence, after the (physical) form which expressed its essential character, has dissolved and disappeared; but as long as it has not acquired (spiritual) self-consciousness and self-knowledge, it is forced, after a time of rest, to reappear in a new form (mask or personality), to resume the process of its further development.1 After the divine principle in man has attained individual (spiritual) self-consciousness and self-knowledge, it requires no more embodiments in (physical) forms, and may, harmoniously united with the *All,* continue to exist as a self-conscious

intelligence.

8. The attainment of spiritual self-consciousness and self-knowledge and the necessarily resulting perfection, therefore involves the attainment of immortality, and the latter can only be acquired by acquiring the former. Only that which is perfect remains; the imperfect is continually subject to change.

9. Although the individual human monad, without (spiritual) self-consciousness and knowledge, may arrive at that state of perfection in the slow course of its evolution, extending perhaps over many millions of years, nevertheless there is no necessity to wait until nature may, perhaps slowly and unaided, accomplish her object, but she may be assisted by the individual will and effort of those who know how to proceed.

10. The *first* necessary requirement for all who desire perfection, is therefore *to know* the laws that rule in the visible and invisible universe, and the attainment of the knowledge involves a study of the constitution of the *Universe* and of the constitution of (the soul of) *Man*.

11. From knowledge springs power, but those who possess knowledge, will be in the possession of something that will not benefit them, unless they desire to put it to some practical use. The *second* requirement is therefore *to will*, and as an individual will, deviating from the direction of the will of universal good, or acting in opposition to the latter, is evil, and can only bring final destruction upon him that exercises it,

consequently the will of the individual must act in accordance with the universal will of God.

12. To act evil is for the majority of men far easier than to do good. Good will and desires to become useful must be made to accomplish some work. To overcome the resistance of evil and to put good into practice requires energy, courage and effort, and the *third* necessary requirement is therefore *to dare* to practice the good which we know and desire.

13. But as a power, after it has once been obtained, may be employed for good or for evil purposes, and as it is not desirable that persons with evil

THE SECRET SIGNS OF THE ROSICRUCIANS

By Franz Hartmann

There are sixteen signs by which a member of the order of the Rosicrucians may be known. He who possesses only a few of those signs is not a member of a very high degree, for the true Rosicrucian possesses them all.

1. *The Rosicrucian is Patient.*

His first and most important victory is the conquest of his own self. It is the victory over the LION, who has bitterly injured some of the best followers of the Rosy Cross. He is not to be vanquished by a fierce and inconsiderate attack made upon him ; but he must be made to surrender to patience and fortitude. The true Rosicrucian tries to overcome his enemies by kindness, and those who hate him by gifts. He heaps not curses, but the burning' fire of love upon their heads. He does not persecute his enemies with the sword, or with faggots, but he suffers the weeds to grow with the wheat until they are both matured, when they will be separated by Nature.

2. *The Rosicrucian is Kind.*

He never appears gloomy or melancholy, or with a scowl or sneer upon his face. He acts kindly and politely towards everybody, and is always ready to render assistance to others. Although he is different from the majority of other people, still he tries to accommodate himself to their ways, habits and manners, as much as his dignity will permit. He is, therefore, an agreeable companion, and knows how to converse with the rich as well as with the poor, and to move among all classes of society so as to command their respect; for he has conquered the bear of vulgarity.

3. *The Rosicrucian knows no* Envy.

Before he is accepted into the order he must go through the terrible ordeal of cutting off the head of the snake of envy ; which is a very difficult labor, because the snake is sly, and easily hides itself in some corner. The true Rosicrucian is always content with his lot, knowing that it is such as he deserves it to be. He never worries about the advantages or riches which others possess, but wishes always the best to everybody. He knows that he will obtain all he deserves, and he cares not if any other person possesses more than he. He expects no favors, but he distributes his favors without any partiality.

4. *The Rosicrucian does not Boast.*

He knows that man is nothing but an instrument in the hands of GOD, and that he can accomplish nothing useful by his own will; the latter being nothing but the will of GOD perverted in man. To GOD he gives all the praise, and to that which is mortal he gives all the blame. He is in no inordinate haste to accomplish a thing, but he waits until he receives his orders from the Master who resides above and within. He is careful what he speaks about, and uses no unhallowed language.

5. *The Rosicrucian is not Vain.*

He proves thereby that there is something real in him, and that he is not like a blown-up bag filled with air. Applause or blame leaves him unaffected, nor does he feel aggrieved if he is .contradicted or encounters contempt. He lives within himself, and enjoys the beauties of his own inner world, but he never desires to show off his possessions, nor to pride himself on any spiritual gifts which he may have attained. The greater his gifts, the greater will be his modesty, and the more will he be willing to be obedient to the law.

6. *The Rosicrucian is not Disorderly.*

He always strives to do his duty, and to act according to the order established by the law. He cares nothing for externalities, nor for ceremonies. The law is written within his heart, and therefore all his thoughts and acts are ruled by it. His respectability is not centered in his external appearance, but in his real being, which may be compared to a root from which all his actions spring. The interior beauty of his soul is reflected upon his exterior, and stamps all his acts with its seal ; the light existing in his heart may be perceived in his eye by an expert ; it is the mirror of the Divine image within.

7. *The Rosicrucian is not Ambitious.*

There is nothing more injurious to spiritual development and expansion of the soul than a narrow mind and a selfish character. The true Rosicrucian always cares much more for the welfare of others than for his own. He has no private or personal interest to defend or foster. He always seeks to do good, and he never avoids any opportunity which may present itself for that purpose.

8. *The Rosicrucian is not Irritable.*

It is evident that a person who works for the benefit of the whole will be hated by those whose personal advantages are not benefited thereby; because selfishness is opposed to magnanimity, and the claims of the few are not always compatible with the interests of the community. The Rosicrucian will therefore be often resisted by narrow-minded and short-sighted people; he will be slandered by calumniators, his motives will be misrepresented, he will be misjudged by the ignorant, ridiculed by the would-be wise, and taunted by the fool. All such proceedings, however, cannot excite or irritate the mind of the true Rosicrucian, nor disturb the divine harmony of his soul; for his faith rests in the perception and knowledge of the truth within himself. The opposition of a thousand ignorant people will not induce him to desist from doing that which he knows to be noble and good, and he will do it even if it should involve the loss of his fortune or of his life. Being able and accustomed to direct his spiritual sight towards the divine, he cannot be deluded by the illusions of matter, but clings to the eternal reality. Being surrounded by angelic influences, and listening to their voices, he is not affected by the noise made by the animals. He lives in the company of those noble beings, who were once men like others, but who have become transfigured, and who are now beyond the reach of the vulgar and low.

9. *The Rosicrucian does not think evil of others.*

Those who think evil of others see merely the evil which exists within themselves reflected and mirrored forth in athers. The Rosicrucian is always willing to recognize in everything that which is good. Tolerance is a virtue by which the Rosicrucian is eminently distinguished from others; and by which he may be known. If a thing appears to be ambiguous, he suspends his judgment about it until he has investigated its nature; but as long as his judgment is not perfect, he is more inclined to form a good opinion than an evil one about everything.

10. *The Rosicrucian loves justice.*

He, however, never sets himself up as a judge over the faults of others, nor does he wish to appear to be wise by censuring the mistakes of others. He does not enjoy gossip, and cares no more about the foolishness committed by others, than he would about the buzzing of a fly or the capers of a monkey. He finds no pleasure in listening to political or personal quarrels, disputations, or mutual recriminations. He cares nothing for the cunningness of a fox, the dissimulation of a crocodile, or the rapacity of a wolf, and is not amused by the stirring up of mud. His nobility of character lifts him up into a sphere far beyond all such trifles and absurdities, and being above the sensual plane, wherein ordinary mortals find their happiness and enjoyment, he lives with those who do not think evil of each other, who do not rejoice about an injustice done to their brother, or make merry about his ignorance, and enjoy his misfortunes. He enjoys the company of those who love the truth, and who are surrounded by the peace and harmony of the spirit.

11. *The Rosicrucian loves the truth.*

There is no devil worse than falsehood and calumny. Ignorance is a nonentity, but falsehood is the substance of evil.

The calumniator rejoices whenever he has found something upon which to base his lies and to make them grow like mountains. Opposed to it is the truth, it being a ray of light from the eternal fountain of GOOD, which has the power to transform man into a divine being. The ROSICRUCIAN seeks, therefore, no other light but the light of truth, and this light he does not enjoy alone, but in company of all who are good and filled with its divine majesty, whether they live on this earth or in the spiritual state; and he enjoys it above all with those who are persecuted, oppressed, and innocent, but who will be saved by the truth.

12. *The Rosicrucian knows how to be silent.*

Those who are false do not love the truth. Those who are foolish do not love wisdom. The true Rosicrucian prefers to enjoy the company of those who can appreciate truth to that of those who would trample it with their feet. He will keep that which he knows locked up within his heart, for in silence is power. As a minister of state does not go about telling to everybody the secrets of the king; so the Rosicrucian does not parade before the public the revelations made to him by the king within, who is nobler and wiser than all the earthly kings and princes; for they only rule by the authority and power derived from Him. His secrecy ceases only when the king commands him to speak, for it is then not he who speaks, but the truth that is speaking through him.

13. *The Rosicrucian believes that which he knows.*

He believes in the immutability of eternal law, and that every cause has a certain effect. He knows that the truth cannot lie, and that the promises made to him by the king will be fulfilled, if he does not himself hinder their fulfilment. He is, therefore, inaccessible to doubt or fear, and puts implicit confidence in the divine principle of truth, which has become alive and conscious within his heart.

14. *The Rosicrucian's hope is firm.*

Spiritual hope is the certain conviction resulting from a knowledge of the law, that the truths recognized by faith will grow and be fulfilled; it is the knowledge of the heart, and very different from the intellectual speculation of the reasoning brain. His faith rests upon the rock of direct perception and cannot be overthrown. He knows that in everything, however evil it may appear to be, there is a germ of good, and he hopes that in the course of evolution that germ will become developed, and thus evil be transformed into good.

15. *The Rosicrucian cannot be vanquished by suffering.*

He knows that there is no light without shadow, no evil without some good, and that strength only grows by resistance. Having once recognized the existence of the Divine principle within everything, external changes are to him of little importance, and do not deserve great attention. His main object is to hold on to his spiritual possessions, and not to lose the crown which he has gained in the battle of life.

16. *The Rosicrucian will always remain a member of his society.*

Names are of little importance. The principle which presides over the Rosicrucian Society is the truth; and he who knows the truth, and follows it in practice, is a member of the society over which the truth practices. If all names were changed and all languages altered, the truth would remain the same ; and he who lives in the truth will live even if all nations should pass away.

These are the sixteen signs of the true Rosicrucians, which have been revealed to a pilgrim by an angel who took away the heart of the pilgrim, leaving in its place a fiery coal, which is now incessantly burning and glowing with love of the universal brotherhood of humanity.

SECRET SIGNS & ROSICRUCIAN RULES

By Paul Sedir

SECRET SIGNS OF AN ADEPT

1. The Rose-Croix is patient.

2. Good.

3. He doesn't know envy.

The Vulgate translates this term by the word Mandragores.

This was revealed to a pilgrim by an angel who removed his heart and replaced it with a burning coal. (Madathanus).

DEVICE OF THE ROSE-CROIX

Ex Deo nascimur. In Jesu morimur. Per Spiritum Sanctum reviviscimus.

ROSICRUCIAN RULES

1. Love God above all.

2. Devote your time to spiritual development.

3. Be completely altruistic.

4. Temperate, modest, energetic and silent.

5. Learn to understand the origin of the metals within you.

6. Guard against pretension.

7. Live in constant adoration of the Supreme Good.

8. Learn the theory before the practice.

9. Exercise charity towards all beings.

10. Read the ancient books of wisdom.

11. Seek to understand their secret sense.

12. Arcana reserved to the Rose-Croix. It is purely interior. (Madathanus).

www.ingramcontent.com/pod-product-compliance
Lightning Source LLC
LaVergne TN
LVHW041458070426
835507LV00009B/670